The Show Must

go On

Olivia Summer Hutcherson

ISBN: 978-1-6847-0798-0 (sc)
ISBN: 978-1-6847-0801-7 (e)

Interior Image Credit: Adriana Montalvo, Vicky Good, Spice Fotor, Rootz Art, Zoe Pappis & Joseph Asbery from Studio 1 Production.

Scripture quotations marked (NIV) are taken from the Holy Bible, New International Version®, NIV®. Copyright © 1973, 1978, 1984, 2011 by Biblica, Inc.™ Used by permission of Zondervan. All rights reserved worldwide. www. zondervan.com The "NIV" and "New International Version" are trademarks registered in the United States Patent and Trademark Office by Biblica, Inc.™

Scripture taken from the New King James Version®. Copyright © 1982 by Thomas Nelson. Used by permission. All rights reserved.

Lulu Publishing Services rev. date: 09/26/2019

Dedication

I would like to dedicate this book to all of the broken souls that still have prisons of pain surrounding them (both internally and externally). If you are reading this right now it is not by chance. It is not a coincidence that your eyes, ears and heart have landed on this page today to remind you of what *really* matters. God has been waiting to do amazing things in your life and He will meet you in the gap if you just let Him in.

The moment we surrender and come to our end, we can start a fresh beginning with Him. My prayer is that these words encourage you one page at a time and one day at a time to use everything that tried to break you as a platform to lift you higher. I have personally found that the only one who could elevate me and sustain the foundation was, is and continues to be Jesus Christ. My decision to follow Him doesn't make me better than anyone else, it just makes me better than I used to be yesterday and for that I am eternally grateful and will dedicate every breath to Him all the days of my life.

Contents

"For I know the thoughts that I think toward you, says the Lord, thoughts of peace and not of evil, to give you a future and a hope. Then you will call upon Me and go and pray to Me, and I will listen to you. And you will seek Me and find Me, when you search for Me with all your heart."

-Jeremiah 29:11-13 (NKJV)

Epigraph

"Each day our life has just begun."
-Olivia Hutcherson

"Compassion is LOVE in action."

"It's ok to climb while you're crying."
-Carl Lentz

Preface

"The Show Must gO On" is a deeply intimate and personal glimpse into the window of a young woman's soul who has spent the last 30 years fighting for her dreams, love, and most recently... her life. Olivia is an accomplished dancer, entertainer, teacher and Breast Cancer Survivor who has been featured on multiple platforms at a high level but falling to her knees is what truly caused her to look up. "Unfortunately or fortunately we must get broken to become open for the light to shine through again sometimes." -Olivia

Olivia's poetry captures the highs and lows of life's many hardships in New York City as a struggling artist, woman, young cancer patient, friend, lover and family member who has dealt with a variety of challenging issues including disease, addiction, relationships, abandonment, abuse and the inner conflict of choosing faith over fear.

Her words are sweet and sensitive but also deeply thought provoking. She is relatable to anyone who may be experiencing suffering and inspiring to those who have lost hope along the way.

Truly a spiritual journey to read her verbal choreography.

Acknowledgment

All glory belongs to God, my personal Savior, Jesus Christ and The Holy Spirit who helped lift my head when the flesh and world failed me. I truly don't know where I would be without my faith. It is NOT religion, it is relationship and it is the most important one in my life.

I'd also like to acknowledge my Mother, Diana Sullivan. You are my heart in human form and the one person I consider my rock. Thank you for your countless acts of sacrifice, kindness, care, love, affection, knowledge, wisdom and leadership taught through example. I cherish you.

To my brother, Robby Hutcherson it has been a long and hard road with you and I but there is no one I would rather share it with. When I look at you I see the laughter and tears of our childhood behind us and I imagine the dreams we have not yet conquered before us. As we walk/dance somewhere in the middle, I believe it's called the *present,* I realize how grateful I am for this gift called family.

To my dear friends, you each blew in at different seasons with a warm summer breeze that comforted me deeply in the middle of my winter. You have all left lasting impressions and been an essential and necessary part of my journey towards healing. Words will never do justice for the memories that live in my heart. There are too many names and organizations to mention here but the ones I am convicted to put in ink will stain this page forever as an outward reflection of my inner gratitude. (In no particular order) they are as follows:

The Rokhlin Family, The Lakhter Family, The Sepiashvili Family, The Duran Family, Pastor Rene Abreu, Hudson Church, The Montalvo Family, Orla Roche, Kelly Millholland, Michael Groberman, Pink Heals, 5 Under 40, David Evangelista, Bonnie Stein, Jemma Everyday, Jose Tutes, Claude Marcel, Karina Saber, Kr3ts, Rootz Art, Ballroom BASE, Mykhaylo Smagin, Aleksandra Gisher, Jani-Joel, Dillon Lehman, Jingjing Lai, George Ciao, Stepping Out Studios, Lori Michaels, Peak PAC NJ, Amy Romero, Kristy Hall, TRIX, Victor Sho, Shirlene Quigley, Broadway Dance Center, Hillsong NYC & Pastor Carl Lentz.

(We haven't met yet but your sermons spoke life into me on my darkest days and this is my personal thank you note. Hope to tell you in real life one day :)

Finally to Mr. Pat Law, an unlikely stranger who showed up at a time where I was down to nothing, God was clearly up to something. You were an angel in disguise that quickly became a blessing and have continued to show your belief in me and my work ever since you heard my story. Our connection was made through a mutual friend, the 1 and only Ms. Vicki Rox. Our bond flourished over time after learning of your love story with your wife, Yonina who also battled through this horrific disease called cancer.

In honor of her and all women who have undergone this mental, physical and spiritual warfare I would like to carve a little piece of history in the sands of time to keep her legacy going. Perhaps we are all in perfect harmony with Yonina's lifelong mission to continue paying it forward. You certainly have by this kind gesture of supporting the publication of my first book. I can not thank you enough. I pray the words that flow off of these pages move your heart and make her feet dance in heaven too!

This is my confession of faith in Jesus name.

Introduction

3 years, an ocean of tears and more times crashing than flowing to make it back to shore but now I'm sure. In fact, I've never been more sure. The journey has just begun, my eyes can see the sun. My head is above water and I'm not drowning anymore in the tears that once suffocated me.

Surrendered and free...I can finally breathe.

I'm really ALIVE, I'm really inside.

The creator of the ocean reminded me how to dance. When I couldn't catch the wave, Living Waters gave me a second chance. I was scraping the floor looking for a piece of me but when I exchanged it for Him I overflowed with peace in me.

Welcome to the greatest show of all...His name is Jesus

I am finally home

Sunshine Girl

There once was a girl

with sun in her hair

She didn't have

a single care

She loved the world

and making friends

She danced and sang

amongst the wind

Always looking

for something new

Under the sky

was where she grew

Stars in her eyes

A smile on her lips 💋

Everyone wanted

to take a sip 🍸

She gave and she gave and then she gave more!!!

Always questioning

What's it All For??? 💭

The more that she learned

the less that she knew 📚

Just craved sharing love

with souls that were true 💕

Perhaps it was wrong

to dream of this life

Where flowers were pink 🌸🌺

and people were kind

But no matter how dark

the clouds were ahead ☁

She always just looked

for the sunshine instead ☼

Losing My Way

ℛ

The deepness of my sadness
has never known such bounds
If these tears could talk
They'd tell you that I drowned

Color has turned to black and white
I can't hear the sound
It seems that I went missing
Don't know when I'll be found

That day will always haunt me
Head hung through Broadway Town
Couldn't make it through the smoke
Twin Towers sad...came crashin down

I'm a lover not a fighter
But picked my gloves up for this round
And I will come out swingin
Even if some blood is found

It hit me like a wave
Ocean blue and all around
So I'll pray til words come back
Gettin Lost and Gettin Found

Double Mastectomy

The most powerful drug in the world is to know that people love you <3

☥

Battling internally
To find the peace
Inside of me
Standing O
To falling knees
Few know what is hurting me
Praying that God has the keys
Release me from life's misery
"Busy" is New York's disease
We feed it that's the irony
Every angel has it's beast
Joy is what I'd like to lease
Just 1 day to live like we
Are fulfilling destiny
A lot of music
Wild and free
Pure until eternity
Original as planted seeds
Building flowers and the trees
Perhaps "I" could become "WE"
I'm finally where I'm meant to be

What a week it has been!!! Just wanted to take a moment to thank some of the special souls who continue to teach me what friendship IS :)

You all own a little piece of my heart. 💔✨💔✨💔✨

#poetrytime #nighttime #justreminiscing #onelove #onelife #bekind #stayfaithful #LivStrong

Friendship IS...

𝕏

Friendship is
A gesture from the heart
Time & Place don't matter
The GIVING is the ART

I have been reminded
In the midst of life's tart
The beauty within strangers
Who filled my broken parts

Like a bullet I was dodging
Out here in the dark
Couldn't trust a soul
Now surrounded by the sparks

I want to thank you all
For shipping friends to my cart
It seems I have an army
Behind these battle scars

Old Friend...

Today I woke up
And realized I'm the same
Still just a girl
Lookin to make a name

I hope to touch the world
And leave it a better place
Help someone feel understood
Because no life is a waste

When I think of happiness
I close my eyes and see your face
2 kids just holding hands
Laughing at the "New York" race

Skipping fast and
Singing loud
Just to know you
Makes me proud :)

I stop for a second
To take it all in
Maybe the journey
Is the win

And although I'm built
Of stars and dreams
My heart slows down on
Central Park's Green

To take off my shoes
Put my feet in the dirt
Music and Popsicles
Take away the hurt

No words necessary
Just a look in the eyes
And it is in this moment
The angels start to cry

Not because they're sad
But rather, there's purpose in the day
God painted a masterpiece
In a single trace

I swear I'm always true and
Do things my own way
But old friend when we're together
There's no time or space

Writing by the pool
#inspired#dontleavemealonewithmythoughts#blankpage
#oldfriend #poetry

(Dedicated to The Lakhter Family)

Welcome to the Poconos

℞

Picture perfect!
No filter needed
Sales and sunshine
My soul is beamin
The smell of salt, cold water, and minnows
Kids just laughing at life's tempo
Rockin docs and waterbugs
So far from home
No tears or drugs
I think this is what they call peace
No need for Facebook
Just sand and trees
Curly hair blowin in the wind
Bikes and bonfires
S'mores with friends
Hot pink nails and chicken fingers
Swimming pools and laughs that linger
Sadness finally begins to undress
Thank you God
For some happiness!

Isn't Manhattan Pretty?

Isn't Manhattan pretty
in the morning when she cries?
The raindrops wash away
the pain she can not hide
The angels spread their wings
above the city's sky
Allow us to reflect
on the seasons of our lives
Isn't Manhattan pretty
sometimes when she cries??
As she stirs up our thoughts
and brings in a new tide
For the clouds are simply dancing
Somewhere up above
While I'm just down here splashing
In my dreams and love
Isn't Manhattan pretty
especially when she cries???
I'm learning it pours hard
right before the light

#poet #lookforthelight #LivStrong

(Dedicated to Michael Groberman)

Bands

Definition of thoughtful
Does way more than a lot though
Makes me feel stronger
Like I'm Livin colossal
Put it in ink
Bands support a good cause yo
Pretty in Pink
Let's dance up to the Stars Grob

To Singapore with Love,

✽

Soulfully connected
Spiritually affected
Masterful to many
Your presence is majestic
Suspended in the air
Time just got arrested
4 years passed us by
But a few talks
Sparked reflection
Ideas about direction
From broken to a blessin
Sometimes the deepest pain
Creates the highest lessons
God can bring correction
If we invite Him to our section
In this life and the next
There is NO greater investment!!!
If you told me of His plans
I would have never guessed it
But my heart is warm like yours
When we're only simply texting

Floor 14

ঽ

Shout Out to the ROCKSTARS
the BRAVE SOULS
and the REBELS

To the women rockin bald heads
Ya'll deserve a medal

As I sat on Floor 14 today
watching every patient
The tears kept rolling down my face
Not sure if I could take it

To the women who are smiling
and holding it together
You are my new heros
Couldn't think of someone better

Behind those silky scarves
and behind the wigs you buy
I see a room of suited soldiers
as I look into your eyes

Shout Out to the ROCKSTARS
the BRAVE SOULS
and the REBELS

May the loved ones that we know
Never have to face this level

For the road is long and hard
and the path is just our own

Thank you to my God
For never leaving me alone

On My Toes...

ℛ

God bless the man
who took a stand
When things got harder
he just held my hand
Reminded me to smile :)
when I said I can't
Kindness in miles
as he marched through the sand
Went by the day
Never the plan
I said "welcome to the jungle"
He said "darlin let's dance!"
Somewhere on my heart <3
is where it is stamped
If you're down for the cause
then I'm in your camp
No words left to say
so I set it in stone
Wherever you are
is where I feel home
Too old for the games
But too young to know
We gon figure it out
We gon put on a show
Both so afraid

So we said let's move slow
But dress rehearsal finished
an hour ago
The best gifts we can give
don't come with bows
So I thank you when I'm fallin
for keepin me on my toes

Blown Away

Never was there ever
a day that would pass
That she didn't treat
like it was her last
Under the lights
she sparkled with class
In diamonds and flowers
Drowning so fast
Counting the days
and thanking her friends
All of my life
Where have you been?
When the music is over
in the city of sin
She just breathes deep
and takes it all in
I swear when it hits
It cuts like a knife
All of the pieces
I'm hiding inside
And there's not enough time

Or words I could say
But the kindness I've witnessed
Just blows me away!!!

Thank you to everyone who brought Summer to my Fall. God bless

#eyeswideshut #isthislovethatimfeeling #LivStrong

Dying to Liv

When I am alone you see
It all swells up inside of me
Pieces flying like debris
But there's no peace in sight to see

Weight is pulling
To my feet
Tears roll down
I hit my knees

Broken doesn't mean I'm beat
But here and now, I taste defeat

I spit it out
No time for weak
Lately my glass has a leak

A life this hard ain't for the meek
So I just smile as I bleed

My heart beats fast before I speak
Words just sound like words to me

The girl I used to know and be
Now has a new identity

If she's hiding
Can you seek?
The spots of light
Behind the grief

Dying to Liv
And just be free
Chemo won't get
The best of me!

More of Him > less of me

'Twas the night before Chemo,

✄

'Twas the night before Chemo,
when all through the house
Not a creature was stirring,
not even a mouse;

Anxious in bed
with nausea and doubt
The princess kept saying
"No tears are allowed!!!"

For what would it change?
Would it make my fear rest?
Would it undo 12 weeks
of IVs and tests?

Would it lighten my load
or undo my stress?
Would it make my hair stay?
Or bring back my breasts?'

Twas the night before Chemo,
so I just crawled in bed
I silenced my thoughts
and then bowed my head

Just speak to your storm
as the old scripture goes
Jesus has got it
under control

#peacebewithyou #speaktoyourstorms #speaklife #reflection
#prayer #chemo #icandoallthingsthroughchristwhostrengthensme
#survivor#breastcancer #breastcancerawareness#bca
#onedayatatime #LivStrong

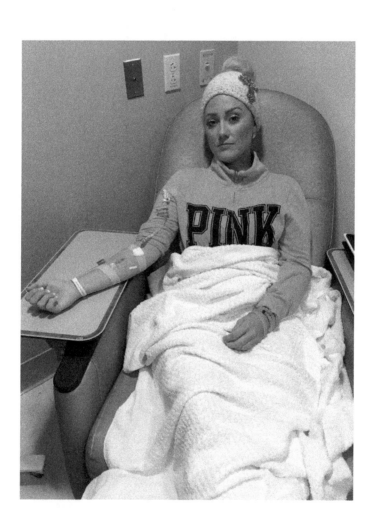

Mama Di

ʡ

She gave me a look
That only a mother could
She gave me a look
That only I understood

She gave me a look
Of sorrow and pain
Because she knows my past
And she knows my rain

She said, "you don't deserve this hell"
And yet we stood there in the storm
I said, "I thought I was a diamond"
But God thought I needed form

So there's pressure
And there's process
And there are days that we must face

There are things that we don't understand
To put new things into place

So I let the water pour
As my mother held my face
In that moment I knew
Everything would be ok

You are the love of my life. The air that I breathe.
Thank you for never, NEVER leaving me.

~Restoration is possible.

Mama Liv

ᛦ

There are NO words I could say
That would finish or even start
To fully describe the place
That you own inside my heart

Lifted me into the light
When I was drowning in the dark
Prayed with me through the struggle
When my faith was feelin far

Told me I'm still magic
When I couldn't wish upon a star
Held me tighter on the days
When loving me was hard

Today I give you all my praise
From the deepest part
That unconditional type tape
That could never pull apart

#Mother'sDayEveryDay #LoveYou #InThisForLife
#FamilyFirst #DearMama #UnconditionalLove

I CAN't

✦

83 days and then it's a wrap
83 days I CAN do this in fact
83 days my body's been hacked
83 days but my soul is intact

11 more weeks of physical pain
Fevers, and aches, and nausea again

11 more weeks of long sleepless nights
But that's when I dream
That's when I write...

The mornings are hard
so that's when I pray
I fall to my knees
and give thanks each day

For this life is a fight
But I came with my gloves
So I CAN and I WILL
Live each day with LOVE

#breastcancer #survivor#chemochronicles #poet
#oldmind#youngheart #soulsearchin

Balloons

Born to shake
Never to break
Fly like the wind
Sky full of paint
Mind full of dreams
Swirling around
Nothing more peaceful
Than watery sounds
Head in the air
Feet on the ground
Saturday morning
I feel my heart pound
Just let it go
Like balloons flying bare
Put on your best smile
We're 1/2 way there

#poet #poetry #writer #optimist #balloons
#loveroflife #letsflyaway #LivStrong 🎈🎈🎈

Strawberry Fields

Ꝕ

Desire inspired
By a mind that won't tire
Touched by your soul
and thoughts of way higher

So much to admire
The words
could perspire

To dream what could be
or even transpire

If I were hired
To write you a song
I'd tell you my stories
All day long

About sunshine
And storms
And clouds in the skies
And then about rainbows
That stem from my eyes

Full of colors
And charming ideas

Where people are sweet
Like strawberry fields

But tonight the only words
words that will do
Is my dear,

I'm thinking of you

Sisterhood

ℛ

Day by day
and through it all
You always help me
To stand tall
Holding hands
with hair that falls
I don't deserve you girls at all
Love you to the moon and back
I swear you keep my heart intact
These aren't lines
Just simply facts
thank you both
for having my back!!!

Buzzed

Anxious but unafraid
The clock just makes me wait
Plucking every hour
Like a new suspicious date

There's no room to hate
Friends hold me everyday
Tell em grab a plate
Tonight we gon exaggerate!!!

Cuz we don't choose our fate
And I wasn't built to break
So buzz me down
and call me mate

I salute my life
and ain't it great?!?!?!

Built on trust
and LOVE
Singing, dancing, writing, hugs

Lift my eyes above
and set it free you peaceful dove...

#phuckcancer #readyforwar #thetimeisnow
#teamworkmakesthedreamwork #baldisbeautiful
#survivor #LivStrong 👊❤️

Til' I Come Back...

ʔ

(Chemo Part II)

I can feel it creepin in
The sickness in my bod again
My back is locked
My knees just shake
The tears roll down
As I break
Cuz I can't seem to hold it in
Not 1 more sec
Not 1 more friend
Just want to hide alone again
Until I pass through every sin
My hands are tied behind my back
My head is cold
It's bald in fact
They want so much
I want to nap
Just let me rest
Til' I come back…

What A Difference 5weeks Makes

(Dedicated to Pastor Rene Abreu of Hudson Church)

Pastor Rene

There's so much that
I want to say
Instead,
I bow my head to pray
To give thanks for
Abundance from above
I've never known
This type of love
You give me hope
Restore my faith
You give me rest
On my hardest days
You teach the word
And live it too
I believe
That it's all true
Call it reborn
Or call it new
The God in me
Sees the God in you
And not for money
Or the car you drive
But reminding us all
That Christ is alive
I dream again

To serve with love
Bring heaven on earth
To the ground from above
I can never pay you back
For the impact that you've made
Restored my soul
After a sentence to the grave
So when I say I love you
Know it's til my dying day
Thank you for being a father
In each and every way 👨‍👦❤️

The Durans

ᛘ

There is power
In your name
No not the kind
That brings on fame
The kind that's kind
The kind that came
Middle of the night
With food and sayings
That tame my mind
That ease my pain
"On the Hudson"
Is more than your domain
It's where you serve
It's where we pray
It's where we start a better day
You change the world
You changed my mind
From Son to Ventanas
Sowing Seeds aligned

Thanksgiving

&

I just woke up
and thought of what to do
I want to start my day
by giving thanks to you

You have touched my heart
and left me feeling new
I'm grateful til the end
for our friendship which is true

Giving and giving
always making it better
I could write for hours
and then until forever

But I'll just tell you here
in the few words that I know
I love you
to the bottom of my dancing toes !!!

Happy Thanksgiving Momager.
I am eternally grateful for your generosity and a spirit that never runs dry.
I appreciate you

Chemo #3

Good night
Good night
Turn out the light
But oh wait 1st
Let's spark it right
My mind will fight
Just not tonight
The body is weak
So careful life
I write, I write
to get it RIGHT
I think I'm on to higher heights
Maybe eyes will take a flight
to Cherry Blossom
Dreams in sight
I'd fly away
like I'm a kite
Before I lay
I pray with might
Because the day
of CHEMO bites
It's #3 of 4

So I...
Will make it through
#LivStrong
Aight!!!

#kyoto #cherryblossomseason #daydreamer #nightthinker

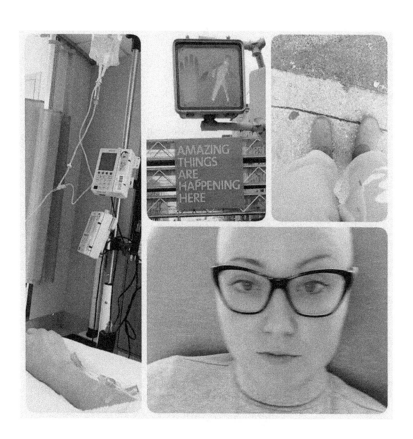

ER

☥

Thankful to say
I made it out ok
Thankful for all
of the people who pray
Thankful to wake up
Each & every day
Thankful for angels
Who bless my pathway
When I fall down
I get back up and say
Not today cancer
Won't block all my rays
Cuz I am a sunshine
Burning and bright
Thankful today
and thankful for life

#stripped #realmoment #emergencyroom #chemosucks
#kickingbreastcancersbutt #LivStrong

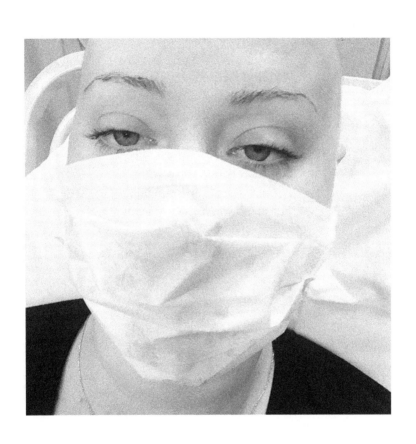

Dear Friends,

⚰

Humbled and grateful
for the messages I've received
Like water for the body
you all help me breathe
Make my load a little lighter
and my smile return again
I may not always respond
but thank you my dear friends
👪👪👪🖤🖤🖤

Where have all the men gone?

&

Where have all the men gone?
the ones that can protect
The men with a little extra
drive and self-respect

The men that love their women
and never turn their back
Where have all the men gone?
Lately there's a lack

Where have all the men gone?
the ones with a beautiful mind
The men with heart and soul
some spirituality would be fine

But I think the men are gone
along with the ladies we once were
I promise if you'll be Him
then my dear, I will be Her

#Kings&Priests #RuleTheNation

McLovin

They just "Like"
No time for LOVIN
They just swipe
Call it screen touchin
Only fakes
Just like McLovin
I overstand
Real stay
Above it

Second Day of Winter

Right now it seems
I'm in the winter of my life
Each and every day
Feels like a fight

My body is weak
My skin is red
My eyes are dark
No hair on my head

Right now it seems
I'm in the winter of my life
Each and every day
Feels like a fight

Little things make me happy
Like a flower or a song
Or having a conversation
So I forget what is wrong

Right now it seems
I'm in the winter of my life
Each and every day
feels like a fight

So if by chance you're busy
Building castles in the sky
I wish you with my heart
All the luck to fly!

But I won't be a check-in
Or a stop along the way
Because I am still worth fighting for
Even on my worst day

World Tour

ᘔ

Tired of wigs
Tired of hats
Tired of silk scarves
tied to the back
Tired of tired
my body's been hacked
Tired of insurance
and the sympathy they lack
Ready for vaca
In my mind I am packed
Done with infusions
now find your way back
What's the "new normal"?
Please tell me the facts
Cuz I'm swimming through the deep end
and this diamond is cracked
I'll smile through the pain
as they all say relax
But shoutout to the brave souls
who take it in racks
Ya'll are my heroes
I mean it to the max
Let's do this walk together
we will make our own map

(1st class back @BDC post chemo! S/O to Carlos Neto #footwork)

All I Want for Christmas (Remix)

I don't want a lot for Christmas
I won't even wish for snow
I just want to feel all better
Out of bed and on my toes
Tell my friends I love them
Give my family a box with bows
Santa Claus just take this pain
I swear no one has to know
Cause I just want to play outside
Get all dressed up and look nice
Maybe even bust a move
Thanks to those who love me
It's what pulls me through!!! ❤

Green Eyes

Twinkle twinkle
little star
Take me back to a time
not as hard
When my eyes were green
and filled with light
And everything we dreamed
was possible in life
Where people were kind
and actually cared
And our inner children
danced around in the air
No need for money
We can pay with our love
Cuz all of my pain
can be cured with a hug
A little music playing
and laughter outside
Holding hands with my people
just building a tribe
No sickness or sadness
No loneliness to heal
And the aches in my body
each night are not real
If you asked me how I'm doing?

There are layers to peel
But each day is a new day
So that's how I feel...

#poet #writer #artist #dreamer #wanderer

Funny Valentine

ஃ

Today we celebrate
the gift of LOVE
So here's to the ones
who help build us up

For life is hard
and the road is long
Thankful to the souls
who help us carry on

The smallest acts of kindness
like a smile or a hug
Can help regrow a nation
with a single touch

It's not what we can get
when trying to reach new heights
But the warmth that we give
that radiates our light

For when I leave this Earth
I hope that it's a better place
And someone breathed easier
in my presence one day

They say protect your heart
so your spirit doesn't fall
But I never lost anything
By watering the flowers on the wall!!!

#poet #writer #artist #flowerchild #lovealwayswins

63

Dear Ms. Gisher,

༊

You give of yourself
You give of your heart
You give life to me
When you teach me of art

I'm thankful in ways
I can not describe
Replaced all my tears
With a smile I can't hide

And when the days
are hard and long
I do not think
I'll carry on

But the gift of dance
Makes it all alright
You've touched my soul
You bring me light...

Thank you for training me during my darkest
days. It will not go forgotten <3

Jingjing

Jingjing Lai
What can I say?
We spent so many
Nights & Days
Of working hard
And then we'd play
But always all along the way
You gave support
You did your part
You gave your smile
Near or far
You and George
House New York stars
Stepping Out
You have my heart

Reconstruction

This morning I awoke
with water in my eyes
Full of gratitude
the war is over inside
Yesterday's surgery
made me realize
That having a healthy body
is the ultimate prize
Still wrapped in bandages
but the cancer has died
And I've never been more sure
that LOVE is ALIVE
They could fill an ocean
with the tears that I've cried
But I would learn to swim
after a headfirst dive
Never knew my own strength
or how hard I could fight
I made it through the storm
with a faith burning bright
Lost some people on the way
who couldn't bear the sight
And yet some surprised me
Who came back day and night
Nothing is too broken

to find its way back to the light
Thank you to the souls
who've touched my heart
and touched my life

Infinity

Sunshine baths ☀️🚼⬛
where children play 🛏️
You held my hand 👫
and told me it's ok 👍
The sky turned blue ✂️
where it once was gray ☂️
You calmed the fear 😦
as you looked my way 👀
No tears allowed ❌😧
just laughed and prayed 🙈
A nice long hug 🙌
to a little Coldplay 🎼
Making jokes 🗣️
calling monkeys gay 🐵🐒
As you sat with me 👯
giving your time away ⚱️
Even rubbed my feet 👣
Now that was brave!!! 🙆
Please hear my heart 👂❤️
and the words I say 💌
For as long as I live 👶
I'll remember this day 💬
Love you for a lifetime ❤️
into in-fi-ni-tay!!! :)

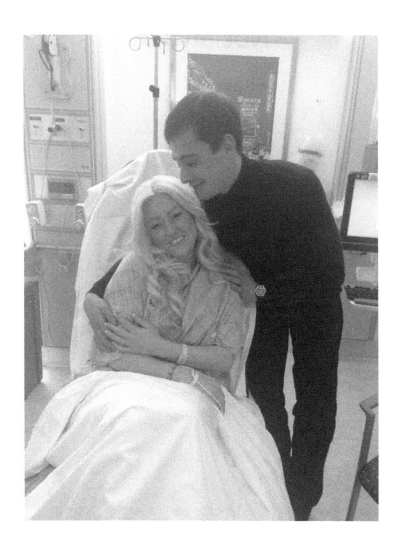

Not Myself

ℛ

With every hour
With every day
With all the words
I do not say
With every song
With every breath
With all the words
Lost in a text
With every heartbeat
With all my air
Tonight I can't breathe
I swear
And I don't know why
But tonight I feel blue
I'm not myself
When I'm not with you...

Some love stories DO belong to the soul and not the body.
We are not here to question when? how? why? and how long?
We simply say thank you for stopping by and reminding me that I
could breathe easier for a few moments in this thing called life.

Burning Building

𝍢

Shoutout to the fireman
the 1 who stole my heart
You brought me back to life
as my building fell apart

He calls me the White House
cuz I light up in the dark
I call him Superman
cuz I'm safe inside his arms

Makes me feel beautiful
healing hands on my scars
Never running from the flames
you go in when times get hard

Remind me there's still good men
beneath the moon and stars
Been awhile since I felt this
you caught me so off guard

Cupid shot his arrow
in a New York City bar
Met you at The Standard
after filming under the stars

73

Wasnt' lookin for love
but it hit me like a dart
God knew what He was doing
when He gave us our start

Good Night Text

All I ever need
is the good night text
Cuz without it
I don't sleep
No...I don't even rest
Got me thinkin of your kiss
When you're workin on BIG red
On the ladder or the streets
I'm your fan in a white dress
Wanna give you what you need
So listen what the album says,
Got me blastin Drake
Cuz baby "you're the best"
Just give me all or nothing
and I will never give you less

Can't Be Friends...

ϙ

Creepin in
Through the cracks
Runnin my heart
Right off track
Lately feelins can't be masked
The most authentic chick
You passed
Never want to become shady
Cuz I'm such a good damn lady
Loyal til the very end
Which is why I can not be your friend

#nosuchthingasfriendswithbenefits

Marilyn & Dean

☗

Thank you for all
that you said last night
My name ain't Roxanne
but I can put on a red light
If we ever made love
you know that I would bite
And I don't even mind
the occasional good fight
Cuz we fight for ourselves
and what we believe
I was in the ring before
Tryna turn "I" into TEAM
Say you're my biggest fan
So let the past be a dream
but I swear I'm wide awake
And things are nothing
like they seem
"The one that got away"
is what I have been deemed
But I have grown a lot
since you first met me
Livin out our best lives
like a movie scene
But I just yelled cut
Cuz I ain't Marilyn
& you ain't Dean

Girl in A Dress

Girl in a dress
No she's not like the rest
Wants to give you her best
Lay her head on your chest

Walk in the grass
Reminisce on the past

Speak with ya
Dream with ya
BE with ya
Breathe with ya

Get lost in your eyes
Forget about goodbyes
Trust in your laugh
And always share ½

But you're just a guy
So you make her cry

Girl in a dress
Said you're just like the rest

I am NOT my Hair

❦

I am NOT my Hair
I'm not what I wear
Clothed in scars and smiles
Come close if you dare

Please handle with care
Because this package is so rare
When they see her walking
They all stop and stare

A spirit you should fear
Because I am still here
Got me screaming out Liv Strong
Like the anthem of the year!!!

Listen to the cheer
I feel my time is near
Shoutout to the good souls
Who helped wipe every tear

Signed yours truly,

From a heart that's so sincere

#latepost #cancersucks #survivor #poet #LivStrong

Slow Down

𝄐

Slow down girl
Don't move too fast
Slow down girl
No need to crash
Slow down girl
Protect your heart
Slow down girl
Go make some art
Slow down girl
They move so fast
Slow down girl
But leave the past
Slow down girl
So you can see
You're THE ONE
They're 2's and 3's

What's Inside...

They say "hurt people, hurt people"
So I aimed my arrow at you
Shooting venom from my mouth
Cupid cried the whole night through

It seems we fell apart
You used to hold me tight like glue
But when the joke was on me,
All emotions flew!!!

In the heat of the moment
I said words that were untrue
When I thought I'd find relief,
It just left me feeling blue

Wish the stars would have aligned
and told me what to do
Guess it caught me so off guard
Because I put my trust in you

Handed over the keys
To a heart that was bruised
You removed so much grief
Perhaps you'll never have a clue

All I'm trying to say,
Is even if we're through
I am deeply sorry
For the way I spoke to you

11months

ǂ

And suddenly it hits me
while I'm lying on my back
How precious our time is
and how quickly it can pass

Today's 11 months
since my body was hacked
By the nastiest disease
this thing called cancer is whack!!!

Brought me to my knees
and stole my money stacks
Sometimes I can't breathe
from the countless flashbacks

Not even my enemy
would I wish this attack
Robbed my nights of sleep
and had me slippin through the cracks

My faith it gives me wings
to fly towards a comeback
So to the fighters keep your head up
Turns out I beat it, raise a flag!!!

#LivStrong #cancersux #bca #staypositive #countyourblessings
#collectmomentsnotthings 👼💜🎗😷👑

40 Bond St.

☦

Lately I've been livin
Each day like my last
I suppose it's only natural
To blame it on the past

They tell me to slow down
But I always move too fast
I swear it all feels like a movie
Now come and meet the cast!

Cuz they all play their role
And we all have a blast
Tagging every picture
Creating new hashtags

If I were a button
The world just likes to mash
But before I rest my head tonight
Let's go and get this cash

#catering #welldonegoodservant #thehustleneverends
#livinthedream #welcometonewyork

Remission

Can I get an intervention?
Cuz I think I failed to mention
I been workin overtime
Like I'm plannin for a pension
Seems that over time the stress built up
I think it's time to bench him
Like the bad boy after school
You know the one that's in detention
Thought that Broadway would be cool
God thought I needed intermission
So I paused then came right back
Think I finally learned to listen
Real life's the greatest teacher
PhD in cancer kickin
We're just catchin and releasin
That old New York City tension
When they see me comin
They will feel that I am different

PS – this is what it looks like
1 year in remission

#saved #poet #poetry #writer #survivor
#cancersucks #betterbecauseofit #smelltheroses #spreadlove
#dowhatmakesyourheartsmile #LivStrong

87

Today!!!

☦

Roll back to the summer
of 2015
Before the nightmares started
and life was still a dream

Just a ball of sunshine
out there on the New York scene
She was lookin for herself
or something close it seemed

I believe the month was June
the air was hot and sticky
In that beautiful white suit
She said, "you better birthday kiss me!!!

Cuz if you don't tonight,
then 1 day you're gonna miss me
And not havin me around
can be a little risky

Tryin to replace me
is like "wine after whiskey"
She was dancin to her own drum
yea those feet were gettin busy

Always flirtin with a good time
she was sure to make ya dizzy

Cuz that little bombshell sparkled
She had magic inside
And some days I can still see her
(if I just close my eyes)

Because that light was shining through her
like the stars up in the sky
She got brighter in the darkness
she got stronger with the tide
Cancer tried to take her peace
you know the devil likes to lie
Real life Beauty & The Beast
they even cut her open wide

All the chemo made her weak
IVs were drippin by her side
Many nights she lost sleep
on her pillow as she cried

From the passengers seat
she learned a lot along the ride
In the middle of the brokenness
she watched 2 worlds collide:

A world full of pain and
A world full of love
A world with compassion and
A world full of drugs
A world full of friendship
from those you can't imagine
A world where there were sisters

Holdin hands in God's mansion
A world full of hospitals
A world full of church
A world full of hugs
to take away the hurt

A world still worth livin in
or at least one where she'd try
Because it's never too late
to start working on your stride

So she was runnin again
her feet were pickin up the pace
Yea she was fightin for gold
in her own Olympic race

She said every day's a gift
so be careful not to waste
Because *my life* was almost taken
But I could not be erased!!!

Every ounce of beauty
quickly got replaced
With baggy shirts and drains
hangin down to my waist

The day I shaved my head
tears were streamin down my face
I swear I could've filled an Ocean
as I cried out salty waves

I swam through every bottle
Tryna drown out that bad taste
I was lookin for myself

but I could not find a trace

Wearin scars like it was fashion
all wrapped up in gauzy lace
I was bleedin on the inside
with a smile on my face

But I straightened out my crown
and got back in the race
And I'm here today to tell you
we're full of miracles and grace

If there's one thing I could share though
I would tell you not to wait
Do it NOW and not tomorrow
cuz we only have TODAY!!!

Rob

Happy Birthday Little Bro!!!
There are some things
That you should know

Like how I miss our random talks
And late afternoon river walks

Maybe I don't tell you enough
But you're the other ½ of me
And I just wanna see you flourish
Into the best man you can be

It seems this year
Has been a struggle
We both have had
A lot to juggle

Like hospitals, cancer, and finding ourselves
It appears we were both put up on a shelf

But the past is the past
So let's celebrate today
It's good to be here with you
Making a way

Sometimes we can't
Always see the end
But as long as I'm breathing
You'll always have a friend

So hold your head high
As your world will advance
You made it to 26
Tonight we will dance!!!

Love your Big lil Sis...Livvy

Door

As I sit here with my ripped feet
planted in the New York grass
My mind begins to drift
to memories from the past

At times it's overwhelming
but it never seems to last
And I can feel my heartbeat
slowing down as they move fast

Reflecting on life
like I'm starin through the glass
Guess that means I'm other side
like the graduating class

PhD's what they should sign
schoolin life where is my cap?
I'm that Derek Jeter cool
always steppin up to bat!!!

So much these eyes have seen
So much good and bad
But I still like to dream
about the things that I don't have

Guess that might make me extreme
which is why I smile when I'm sad
But don't take me for granted
when I'm priority stack

And maybe on a Friday or the "right day"
he will come
Suited up in all God's armor
more protection than a gun

And we will have a union
built on friendship and trust
You know that higher level
Body, mind, and soul type lust

But I can't look
and I can't hope
and I can't pray anymore

And you're always welcome in or out
But don't stand in my door

#yourstruly #poet #poetry #dancersfeet
#imanartistandimsensitiveaboutmyshit #centralpark 🤟🎼👹🏚️💃🗳️❤️

Italy!!!!

❦

As I open my eyes this morning
I have a smile on my face
Because this time last year
My smile almost got erased
So many salty tears
I filled an ocean as I laid
But I won't waste another minute
On all those yesterdays
I promised myself when I was better
I would go to a magical place
Where there's water and nice weather
And lots of wine to taste
I would cherish every moment
Cuz there's a treasure in each day
So arrivederci America
Italy I'm on my way!!!

#survivor #optimist #thingsdogetbetter #fallequinox
#timetoharvest #bringinglightandloveallday

Table for 1

ጸ

"Table for 1 please"
that's what she said
I had to go across the world
to get some peace in my head
Sometimes in life
we must stop feeding and be fed
Cuz if everything is balance
then it's time for me to "med"
Not medicate, but rather meditate
Put my feet back on the ground
let my soul elevate
And there's no need for tape
cuz there's nothing to hold together
I'm as free as a bird
watch me fly with all my feathers

#poet #poetry #italy #reflect ❤

Confessions from Tinker Bell

ℛ

So alone
Yet quite ok
Lately I seem
To like my space

Time to reflect
Time to just think
Friends call me spirit,
They're callin me Tink

Cuz I like to fly around
And see the world above
From all the way up here
I'm learning self-love

There's no judgement to be made
And no fear that won't pass
With wings this strong
It's impossible to crash

There's this new sense of power
And it comes from within
And if I didn't know me now,
I'd want to be my friend

Not because I'm cool
Or wear the latest fashion
But if soul had a team
I would be the captain

Sometimes they say
That I feel too much
I just smile and reply
"Maybe you don't feel enough!"

Cuz we have 1 life to live
So cut me til I bleed
I'll still come out smiling
Watch me sparkle in the breeze

Sometimes in life
We drop to our knees
But "Where there is life, there is hope"
At least that's how my tattoo reads :)

So keep your head up people
It's not as bad as it may seem
You're welcome in advance
For Confessions from Tink

Dear Mr. Minoan Lines,

☗

You set me back
20 hours in time!!!
Have me reconsidering
Greek airlines
Cuz this part of the trip
is breakin my spine :/
Bus rides
and taxis
and ferrys
and trains
Uncomfortable sleep
and losin my planes
Thank God for Antonio
who walked down the lane
With a charger, and pizza,
and coffee for pain
Cuz I haven't slept at all
and it's cold here on deck
The seats are all broken
and I have a stiff neck
But I'm done complaining
just needed to vent

Thank you little red book
for just listenin

#adventureswitholivia #writer #poet #greecetorome
#almosthome #withthislittleredbookimneveralone 📕🖋️

Straddle

I learned during travel
The layers unravel
Find out who you are
While removing the gravel

A moment to breathe and
Jump off of the saddle
Pick up a cold drink
And put down the battle

Cuz we're not machines
Just built to paddle
In fact we should strive
For balance so straddle

Straddle the line
And let the peace in
Straddle your fears
And make a new friend

Straddle your title
You're more than 1 thing
Straddle your heart
And open your brain

Cuz there's more to life
Than money and fame
But they have it all wrong
And our world is in pain

On my next business card
Put "Kindness" as my name
Then maybe we can have
An honest exchange

No egos
No masks
No need for the games

I suppose I lost a lot
But something else was gained
So wherever I go
I paint my love stains

With 1 simple hope...
Leave em better than they came ❤

Spark

ጸ

This morning
I had a conversation
With a man who produced
Some stimulation
Gave my mind wings
Into elevation
Said he was ruling the world
Now that's inspiration!!!
Spoke of dreams
To have a better Nation
But it starts at home
With our dedication
So let's start a team
Instead of separation
In fact maybe "WE"
Could have some rules just breakin
Cuz I don't like the system
Here right now
Tryna find some truth
In the lost and found
Maybe reach the youth
With my words and sound
My life could be the proof
Right here on the ground
But it's not about me

It's about us
Not about the dancin
But the hearts that we touch
If art is just a vehicle
Then where are we all drivin?
Seems the purpose of it all
Is no longer defining
Cuz we're livin through a screen
Built on likes and views
In fact this whole generation
Is just brainwashed and used

Placing our value
On which way we swipe
And most of you out there
Won't read this tonight
Cuz you'd rather see a selfie
Of me in a two piece
Then read these words of wisdom
Penciled in my notebook sheets
And I can't change the world
But I hope to spark the mind
Of the genius that will
Make it better in time

#poet #poetry #theworldwelivein #innovators #letsmakeachange 🌍

Garden of We

If children are the future
Then let us plant the seeds
So we can grow a garden
Full of flowers and trees
Where the heart is always open
And the mind is always free
You're my brother
You're my sister
Never I
Always WE

#reachyourpeak #peakpacnj #dance #teacher #youthisthefuture 👨‍👩‍👧💙🐾♪♪

Elections

ρ

God please use me
To be an instrument of peace
God please use me
To silence violence in the streets
God please use me
I'm on my hands and knees
God please use me
To love the world back to WE

Dear Mr. President,

ჯ

Out here livin life
On a day-to-day basis
Said Dear Mr. President,
You can NOT erase us!!!
Last time that I checked
There's nothin equal
Bout a racist
Up in Trump Tower
So that you don't
Have to face us
Down here on the ground
We're just fightin 4 our places
America the great
Ain't so great when you disgrace us
I can feel my heart
Beatin strong
Call it BASE
Tryna smile
Through the struggle
Think that's what
They call grace
Take our healthcare
Take our freedom
"Both sides guilty"
What a waste

Of the progress
MLK made
Way back in the day
But you don't own our spirits
Choosin LOVE over hate
Respondin to the darkness
With more light inside each day

#prayforourcountry 🙏❤️☹️

Spread Love

With all the violence
in the world
I pray that we
don't lose our way

With all the hatred
in the streets
I ask that we
don't turn away

With all the children
that we teach
I hope it's kind words
that we say

With all the feelings
of defeat
Let's fight
to spread some love today

So live it up
The time is now
Just take a hand
I'll show you how

One world
One life
And WE are 1
So let's unite
And have some fun!

A Girl Like You

ɸ

A girl like you
Should not be here
A girl like you
Is always dear
A girl like you
No need for fear
A girl like you
Is sun and cheer
A girl like you
With sparkly eyes
Now go and chase
your rainbow skies!

Mahalo

ȣ

And lately I've been drinkin
like there's a message in a bottle
Funny I'm the leader
that they all wanna follow
Cuz most days I just bleed
from this life that's hard to swallow
Then I drop down to my knees
givin thanks to my Father
Cuz He placed faith in me
that helps me deal with all my sorrows
Not that 1 night stand type,
the kind that lasts until tomorrow
That means I own it
never leased or even borrowed
Perfect peace inside the storm
I believe the right term is mahalo

Gains

ℛ

Dear Mr. Surgeon,

Don't cha know I'm hurtin
Pullin back the curtain
Said "I should be alerted"
Pain beneath the skin
Is carried heavy like a burden
Thought this shit was through
But that cancer just be lurkin
All these little boys out here
Kinda got me smirkin
Cuz they worried bout their "gains"
While I just hope the treatment's workin

Clarity

Clarity clarity
Nothin seems fair to me
World upside down
Can someone come carry me?

Wings clipped, no parakeet
Life has just buried me
I'm not a charity
More like a fairy see

Spirit is all I breathe
Lost while I swallow dreams
Searchin & scrapin
The mountains and hollow seas

Discoverin all of me
"Be all that you can be"
I just need love
And a soul that can see see me

Humility

ঽ

Pac said,

"there will be peace on earth
when the earth falls to pieces"
therefore I pray
for humble and weakness

for when I am weak
then He is strong
and we can start again
and write a new song

show us the way
for we're lost in the streets
like a cat that is stray
who is hungry
no eats

I feel the disease
it is wrapped
in our sheets

disease of lonely
disease of pain
disease of trying

to numb our way
disease of no love
solitary confinement
prisons are built
where there's lack of kindness

so I reach to you
when I can't hear me

put me in a box
because you fear me

love is the answer
when how to
get near me

Sign it in tears,

He makes me strong
when I'm weary

"But he said to me, "My grace is sufficient for you, for my power is made perfect in weakness." Therefore I will boast all the more gladly about my weaknesses, so that Christ's power may rest on me. That is why, for Christ's sake, I delight in weaknesses, in insults, in hardships, in persecutions, in difficulties. For when I am weak, then I am strong."

-2 Corinthians 12:9-11(NIV)

BE

ℛ

When's it my turn?
I've already learned
More than I need to know
Haven't they seen me grow?

God talk to me
Help me to see
What I should do
Who I should BE

Turkey Day

ℛ

You can find me where the love is
under the New York City sky
And I don't need Thanksgiving
to be thankful for my life
If beauty's in the eye of the beholder
I guess mine are open wide
And I can tell the difference
Between what's real and what's disguised
Each day there's so much gratitude
sometimes it makes me cry
And from this little fire escape
I feel like I could fly
When it all gets too heavy
I just look up to the sky
And thank God for the darkness
Because it made me chase the light

Fallen Fruit

Her tree was bare
With fallen fruit
Scarred and Bruised
Down to the root

The branches broke
Blood on the leaves
The vines of life
Grabbed on to squeeze

Lowered eyes
Her crown just dropped
It seemed her beating heart
Had stopped

Winter came
And took the sun
Nowhere to go
Nowhere to run

She lost her words
She lost her way
Her wings were clipped
She could not sway

She lost her mind
She was a beast
Beautiful chaos
Inside her sheets

Come close wild ones
If you dare
Can't imagine
All her scares

Ain't nothing bout this
Thing that's fair
I challenge someone
Out there to care

The tears she swallowed
Choked her gray
She bowed her head
Began to pray

This was new
That's no surprise
The body of youth
Dove inside

Clingin on
To spiritual peace
Olives blossomed
From her tree

She was dancin and singin
In the breeze

For the first time ever
She was free

Everything changed
With the tide
God's plans were bigger
Than she realized

Suddenly she paused, paralyzed
Began to heal, she was alive
But in order for new flowers to arrive
First the old me had to die

River

ঽ

Inspired by Galen Hooks Choreography while undergoing treatment

She's a woman
She's a lover
She's a fighter
Undercover
She takes heat and then recovers
Planted seeds, from her Mother
Willow weeps
But she discovers
Deeper peace than the others
Cuz she seeks
The 1 above her
On her knees
As the world shoves her
She can feel
The darkness hover
Yet the white doves
Seem to flutter
Sunlight peekin
Through the shutters
Busy bee
The honey's smothered
Her smile breathes
Life into others

There is hope
Beyond what cut her
She is me and all my sisters
Watch us dance along the RIVER

#RiverChallenge

Montego Bay

ℛ

Too old to be young
Too young to be old
Dying to live
Cuz life got put on hold

I guess some would say
I'm shiny like gold
That's just light pushin through
Ever crack where I fold

Been runnin so fast
Forgot all I've been told
So I lead with my heart
Put your hands on my soul

No it's not the type
To be purchased or sold
It's chicken noodle
Keep you warm when it's cold

And these words are strong
But God has been bold
Shaping the masterpiece
To His perfect mold

Not effortlessly
Patience takes a toll
But today I relax
Along the Montego Bay stroll

#grateful #blessed #beautyinthestruggle#camealongway
#colorsofjamaica#montegobay #poet #poetry 🏞️🧍🌸🌺🌸🌍🍹

Adri

☒

Like a warm breeze
Like a cool sip
Like my favorite jeans
With too many rips
Like a leather jacket
With a floral dress
Or Doc Martens after heels
Like Colombian coffee in the morning
While writing over Chillhop feels
Like Jamming in the park
Like making real life art
Like Hillsong every Sunday
And wishing on the stars
Like every single ending
Becoming our new START
You're a friend that I treasure
And I pray we never snart (lol)

#insidejokenumber572

Lost & Found

Lookin 4 some feelins
In the lost and found
I thought I told ya
LOVE's a VERB and baby
Not a noun
And I can hear my heart
Beatin like an ultrasound
Lyrics to my soul
Rooted in what's underground
That means feel me
Don't just see me
Cuz I'm not around
Busy healin every piece
I hide behind the gowns
I call her beauty and the beast
That double sided crown
But lately I'm just doin me
So I don't have no frowns
Keep it movin in the streets
My head is never down
He said my smile gets him high
When he's feelin down
I told him
I just chase the light
When I'm here in town

Bumpin PAC everyday
Because I get around
And NO!
Not in that way
But yea I lay it down
Buildin bricks to the stars
Til they lay me down
Telescope
Please don't choke
Cuz now I'm gettin found
What?!
I was lost
But now I'm gettin found

#BornAgain #freestyle

The End

ℛ

So as a goddess
I am called to speak the poetry bit
Had me believin you were true
Damn I knew not to trip
Took me high then dropped me low
Between your fingers I slipped
Seems I thought this was love
Am I my losin my grip?
Something happened though
Cuz overnight
Babe you just flipped
Breathe me in
and blow me out
I'll be your favorite hit
Smoke me slow
and choke me down
You know the po-te-ne-nt shit
I call this love on the rocks
You got me drunk
and then dipped
But I'm a miracle
and spiritual
Have your memory lit
Scream my name in your sleep
You know you'd die without LIV

Put it all on the table
As feelins flow from your lips
Locked my heart in a jar
No need for you to break in
So you can knock
and you can try
Your very best to get in

But there's no use
Cuz broken hearts
Won't be broken again
Bleedin love all on your hands
Like a beautiful sin
I heard it stop
The plug was pulled
I guess that this is
THE END

This is THE END
This is THE END
You were never a friend
Ooo Ooo Ooo

Good girl
bad guy
Good girl
wrong time
Good heart
out her mind
Somethin spiritually divine

She like her music
She like her wine
Workin patience
overtime
While she masters
every line
No
not the bumpy kind!!!

White on her teeth
I call it shine
Bling on her smile
will leave ya blind
Wicked cool and crazy kind
She told me everything's fine

Everything's fine
Everything's fine
Yea Everything's fine
My compass Jesus
sent a sign

He said
"Let it go this time"
So … I'm lettin go this time
And this is THE END
Ooo Ooo Ooo

(Dedicated to Handschin)

Ry Bread

ᕼ

"I would face it all again
To have a friendship like this."
Are words I will NEVER forget

Bonded by broken pieces
Of what cancer tried to rip

There were days we didn't speak
And marks we couldn't meet

But the 1 thing we had in common
Was conquering defeat!

*"Yet in all these things we are more than conquerors
through Him who loved us."*

-Romans 8:37 (NKJV)

Master Plan

☦

It all started at the Farmer's Market...

I believe God
is workin a master plan
Maybe that's the reason
I haven't found another man

Cuz it has been years
of things I don't understand
But every time I'm with you
I'm on my knees and hands

Giving thanks in prayer
for the love that you grant
Take away my breath
take me to another land

And we don't even leave the room
But I can hear the band
Every time that we link up
it's a celebration dance

Something like a concert
I could be your biggest fan

Wanna tease you
Wanna please you
Wanna hug you
Hold your hand

So if God is Love
And Love is God
I thank you in advance

It was worth the wait
Sign my heart across the sand

Fireworks

If it's real this time Lord,
Then please don't let it fade
Cuz from the moment that we met
My days turned into brighter days

Every word tucked in my heart
Are the words he goes to say
Every seed that was planted
Has suddenly come out to play

Flowers dancin in the breeze
Joy is washin over me
I finally understand
Why all the others had to leave

I wanna love him till forever
But I'll just start with today
I wanna spend our lives together
'Til our hair turns gray

Haven't felt this in a long time
Won't compare him cuz it's new
Letting go of the past
I believe our future's true

Mister Deen

ℛ

I'll break every wall
And every chain
Til we get back
To the root of your name
"Gift of God"
Is how you came
Delivered to create
And rearrange
Pieces into peace
A masterpiece of pain
A big old world
With no one to blame
Lately I listen,
Pause and refrain
To the words that you say
To the words that just lay
Between the sheets
Of present and past
Between the layers
Of feelings and facts
2 ears
1 mouth
No agenda in place
But each day and night
I can not erase

Your scent from my skin
Your voice from my head
Your eyes from my memory
Your touch in the bed
Fingertips grip my hips
With the morning sun
Loose lips under the moon
Always starts at 1
With stories
And glory
And dreams
And plans
Memories of exes
And family land
But none of it matters
When I'm in your arms
Silenced by the warmth
I prayed for so long
Eternal
Internal
Sunshine in my journal
You're taking up space
That didn't exist
I'm making room
I can not resist
The silence is violent
Whenever you're away
Sometimes I lose
The right things to say
Or have a response
That's sometimes delayed
Better than reacting
Learned that the hard way
So I stop, I think, I try to reflect

Never wanna say
Anything I'll regret
So I focus on me
I surrender, I breathe
Only answer for our future
Is turn I into We
All you have to do
Is use your faith and believe
Our best days are ahead of us
Good night Mister Deen

Sleeping Together

In the city that never sleeps
I wanna sleep next to you
When I said that last week
Every word was true

Perhaps it's hard for you to see
But all of this is so brand new
So excuse the sides of me
That don't know what to do

I've been hiding under covers
Cuz the chaos wasn't through
Can't silence all the thoughts
That linger in my rear view

Never saw you as a friend
Although I want to grow that too
See forever in your eyes
With a child or maybe two

I apologize for last night
If I came off as confused
But it appears to me
That my trust's a little bruised

I'm working on myself
And trying every day
To be the best woman
A man like you could pray

For
Stay
more
Don't
GO!
I don't
know???
What our title is
Just know I wanna live
Morning and night
And every single day
Wanna know everything about you
Believe the words you say

Hug you,
Love you,
Kiss you,
Touch you
Never put another man above you

Unless it's God
Because I see Him in you
He loves a persistent heart
And my love is never through

So don't think it is that easy
To just walk away
I will fight like I always do
Past all the gray

Get some rest for now
I want to let this breathe
But never will I ever
Just get up and leave

The reason there's no name
Is cuz we're limitless you see
But from the moment that we met
You're the only place I want to be

Phases

ℛ

I don't know
The words to say 💭
And if you don't
Well then I'll pray 🙏
For hope to see
A better day 🌈
Where pain leads to purpose
It's not a waste 🗑
Cuz storms don't last
They wash away ☂
What's not meant
for you or me 💨
Gonna love you through it
If I may 💔
I know you know
He knows the way 💡
So we're not layin down today
Gonna come outside with Oli and stay ☀
Above it all and past the gray
Our enemies teach us
What we're made
Of
Is enough 💪
Let's just let fate 🔥
Take us to our des-ti-nay 🦋

If the light falls out ✨
I'll remind you to walk 👣
Not by sight 🌀
But by your faith
The moon is still the moon ⚪
In every phase 🌓
No one 👳‍♀️
No one 👳‍♂️
Can take that away!!!
Peace is yours ✋
Unlock the cage 🔑
Society built on culture's way
Repaint the canvas 🎨
It's ours to trace
Deeper than a pretty face 🎭
Deen and Liv
Will rule the place 🌀
Under the sky
With no brakes 🚗
Our dreams
Will change the world 🌍
One day!!!
What's ours will never
Be erased ▬
And if you're here
Or far away ✈️
My spirit sees yours
Past time and space 🔭
Just know I love
What's at your base 🖤

Woke

ℛ

I am thankful for ALL
you woke up inside of me
For finding the pieces
I hide in me
For seeing the different sides of me
For staying
When others don't ride with me
You bring out the lows and highs in me
Never been quite this off key
No balance in my life
when you're not with me
At the end of the night
You're where I wanna be
At the end of my life
I want you near to me
Thankful for the man
I saw and see
Getting better with time
Making history
I love you in ink
Make it clear to see
Please manage your anger
So I can be WE
Been lookin my whole life
For who's in front of me

Point Pleasant

I'm not sleeping
I'm breathing
Trying to hear myself
Trying to hear the wealth
Of wisdom in the *silence*
And knowing what to respond to
It's strong too
Cuz I ALWAYS have something to say
But after last night
And another day
Of fighting
I'm writing
In the stillness of my room
There is no longer room
For anything that is NOT true
If LOVE doesn't live here
Than neither do I
And you can take your dresses back
Under the sky
Cuz it will never buy
What I'm looking for
I don't look no more
Because I found it in me
Not co-signing dysfunction
Just to say "we"

Love Yourself

It seems to me
That currently
We're in a state
Of EMERGENCY!!!

My definition of currency
Is kindness, compassion, and unity

But every time I start to breathe
It all builds up inside of me
This life it knocks me to my knees
And challenges my sanity

So much that I have had to see
And still don't understand DISease

I stand back up
Past under me
Hurricane
Can you feel the breeze?

The good times
I would like to freeze
But it never lasts
With you and me

How can we find
Harmony?
When your voice drowns out
My every key

The world slows down
Wrapped up in sheets
We fly as high as
Birds and bees

Your touch was just like
Ecstasy
Unlocked the gate
To body grief

It seems you had the
Master key
Released yourself
Inside of me

Pieces from the past
But there's no peace
And I'm so tired
Of losing sleep

I stitched and stitched
Where you belittled me
Learn to love yourself
And I'll go love me

Carved

🎗

How do I undo
The memories carved in my heart?
Like crying in the hospital chair
As you hugged me while I fell apart 😣

On nights like tonight,
I'm not sure if it's the end or a fresh start
But every time I leave you
It hurts for me to part 💔

Exhale

ༀ

She said the only time is hurts
Is every time I breathe
And I keep that head high
But every night I hit my knees

I wish I could teach him
About the spirit that lives in me
Like how I turned the darkness
Into a summer breeze

Although I am a poet
Words are always cheap
So save that beautiful melody
And show me some deeds

You weren't somethin I wanted
More like a NEED
And every moment apart
Is a moment I bleed

I've searched every corner
And scraped each city block
Watched the old couple walk home
And felt my heart stop

Cuz every hour I'm busy
It's doing nothin at all
And if you're not in my landscape
Then this water can't Fall

And maybe it's an illusion
You know I like to dream
But I'd rather stay alone
If you're not on my team

So when they ask me what I want
I tell em nothin at all
I'll keep searchin for LOVE
Inside these self built walls

Still

And I will NEVER apologize
for being myself
Only guilty of caring
For what my heart once felt
It's time to suck it up though
And tighten the belt
Looks like these are the cards
That I have been dealt
And I'll NEVER understand
all the suffering and pain
I may have lost my mind
But something else was gained
For every road I went off
I found another path
Taking me deeper
As I swam through every crack
And I'm not the type
To ever turn my back
But not even an angel
Could help you unpack
All the demons in your mind
Turned opinions
to facts
And I just want happiness
That might even last

So I lift it up to my Father
And let the good Lord fight
And for the first time in a long time
I am still tonight

"The Lord will fight for you; you need only to be still."
-Exodus 14:14 (NIV)

Loco

Ж

Yes you're a little LOCO
And call too many times
But sometimes to get your point across
You had to cross the line

I've broken every rule with you
And yet somehow it was fine
I used to lead with my feelings
But now I choose my mind

Created so many memories
My heart couldn't seem to unwind
But your jealousy spilled out
And crushed the light divine

Used to say "I'd choose you in this lifetime
And the next one too
Because the God inside of me
Saw the God inside of you"

I once called you my addiction
But I don't believe that's fair
You were more like an element missing
And now I'm without air

Or maybe like a fire
Which is why I kept getting burned
"Say something" is a song
But in real life it's my turn

The silence is my response
And darling it's getting loud
Your violent tongue broke us apart
Just thought you should know now

Us

☥

I love you
More than words
And then
I love you more than that
I will always fight for you
And step up with my bat
For this life has simply started
And the old us has died
Only time for happiness
There's no need to cry
Ends are just beginnings
To what has yet to come
And you are a masterpiece
That God has just begun
So lift your spirits and your head
Always know that you are loved
And we can do anything
Cuz it's never you
It's always US ♥

"I can do all things through Christ who strengthens me."

-Philippians 4:13 (NKJV)

A Time

ૠ

There's a time to pause
There's a time to stop
There's a time to see
You've grown a lot!!!

There's a time to laugh
There's a time to cry
There's a time to let
the old tears dry

There's a time to breathe
There's a time for hugs
There's a time to know
that you're ENOUGH

There's a time to let
the light shine through
and realize the brokenness
isn't all of you

There's a time to curl your hair
There's a time for a red lip
There's a time for some dancing
After your whole world has flipped

There's a time for some joy
And the time is right now!
We stand up, we love again, and
we start again somehow

#poet #poetry #lyricstomysoul #igotthemoves 🎧🎤❤️🕺🎼

Journey to Peace

I'm on a journey
to the other side
Of a peaceful place
where I don't have to hide
Unafraid to shine or breathe
I exhale, I am free
From all your wrath and questions and rage
I'm next chapter
4get new page
30 is gonna be my new age
Your disrespect
was closure
To the war that was waged
Between the mind and the heart
There is no end
There is no start
Couldn't breathe when we were apart
But it's time for me
To press restart

Restart

ℛ

And maybe I never learn
Cuz I'm far too sentimental
Feels like you own my heart
I never liked us as a rental

Can't even sleep @ night
Cuz you are heavy on my mental
The only thing I ask
Is that this time, you please be gentle

Cuz I'm too old for the games
I'm too hurt for more pain
I'm peaceful by myself
But I still dream of your last name

Truth is,
You never left my mind
Sign it in ink across my heart
Told me that night after the Farmer's Market
Our LOVE was written in the stars

Even then I wanted to believe
In all that WE are
But then life happened
And things just got so hard :(

Darling please have faith in me
I have never been too far
Love you until eternity
But I can't wash away the scars

"The one who breaks you
will NOT fix you"
I can hear my Mother start
I pray one day
I teach myself
to love myself this hard

Psalms 147:3 (NIV)

"He heals the brokenhearted
and binds up their wounds."

Messy lips
And eyes that drip
Outside the lines
And fingertips
Of swipes and grips
And fights to get
To the bottom of your darkness
When the jealousy hits

You rip and rip
Til you pull me apart
There is no end
There is no start

There is no twinkle in my star
Attack my soul
And then my heart

Cupid hit us
With his dart

I bleed, can't breathe

I'm fading far

My health's at risk
I'm off the cliff

You cut the cord
Then cried I slipped

DV Line

ℛ

Look at all these women
In the domestic violence line
Send us to Room 104
And tell us to "take our time"
"It's gonna be a long day
So don't make any plans"
When did we all fall victim
To the violence of a man?

Take it Away

ጸ

I get sad, I cry
I get mad, I try
To laugh
And sing
And dance around
And sometimes I even drop my crown!
I make mistakes, I slip, I fall
I seek comfort in anything that will heal me at all
At least for the moment
I'm taken away
From the pain of my memories
I fight night and day

#flashbacks #ptsd

Undo

ጸ

I love you
I don't want to

Cycles

ʁ

Talking hurts
Not talking hurts
Hearing everyone I love
Tell me NOT to love you hurts

And most of all...
Having the man I love most
Love me and hurt me in vicious cycles
Has broken and destroyed my trust

It is all destruction
You're right,
None of it is fair

I am trying to heal every second
But I can't!!!
Because I'm still attached
And involving myself to the source of pain and pleasure

It is hard to describe
Am I dead or alive?
I don't know anymore
I just want to cry

Soul Ties

I throw myself in the fire
Then cry when I get burned
And I can teach my mind
But my heart never learns

My feet keep on moving
And the world will always turn
But when you're not next to me
I feel my soul yearn

For what only you could do
Like a robber you broke through
Some days I really really
Don't know what to do

Because each night my body
Is only craving you

Activate me
Stimulate me
Generate me
Feed me/Plate me

Nourish me
Then take me

Take me
Take me

To the pieces deep in you
Through the portals where only I get through

Is it love
or
Addiction?

Is it worth what we are riskin?

Speak of multiplying

Don't subtract me -
No division

Cuz every time
You leave my space
I am busy
Counting days

Noise gets louder
In my head
There's a pain
My body dreads

That only you
Can take away
Will you hurt me?
Or keep me safe?

I don't know
And I don't care

Life without you
Is NO AIR

So I'll keep choking
Asthma attack
Will love kill us
Or will love last?

Truly only
Time will tell
Someone help me
My heart fell

Laying Hands

ʾ

It is finished
It never started
The day you hit me
Our souls were parted

And now it hits me
My sin restarted
The moment I let you back in again
RETARDED

So who's the sick one?
You or me?
Am I walking in the flesh?
Or the Trinity?

My brother schooled me today
And reminded me of He
Holy Spirit silenced
The lack of love in me

Because my scars made me forget
I'm a daughter of The King
Your touch was what I wanted
But prayer is what I need

Weakness is always
What the enemy will feed
But that is not my portion
I choose The Prince of Peace

So I lift my hands
And speak life with my mouth
This body is the temple
To God's sacred house

#can'ttouchthis

11/12

୫

You said our love was eternal
But even the flowers die
So after 11 months of gardening
On the 12th one I won't try

I gave you all I had to give
But last night my tears ran dry
This is a poem to myself

Dear Liv,
There's good in goodbye

Swerve

Try to turn me down
Try to shut me out
Silencing my voice
Sometimes I wanna to shout!!!
Please don't feed my fears
Again you're gettin loud?
I'm just bein me
Tryna make God proud
Pray for eyes to see
But you just poked mine out
I turn I to we
But you just dig me out
When will I be free?
From this toxic route
Your hateful words
Are tied around my mouth
You turned our HOME
Into a house
The bruises fade
But I'm filled with doubt
The next man shouldn't pay
For the hate you vowed
Jesus take the wheel
And get me out

Heal Me

ߙ

Falling out of a toxic relationship for the 99ᵗʰ time.
What's important is that you stand 100.

I can feel it creepin in
There I go
I'm numb again
Spacing out
Between the lines
For 7 months
I've said "I'm fine"
Ironically, that's the same # of times
That women return
to their partners in crime
Of abuse to the body & feminine divine
Then I wonder why
I can't unwind
Nights are long
And mornings aren't mine
I'm a slave to the flashbacks
That run through my mind
Doctors diagnosed me
Told me to count my time
But "No weapon formed against me Shall prosper "
Is STILL my favorite line
Isaiah 54:17 always allows me

A safe space to find
A moment of peace
A moment of release
A moment to breathe
So I breathe & I breathe

I apply oil and light candles
And try to forget your face
I turn on pink light crystals
And undo every trace
I remember to forget you
I wash myself in the word
I pray
I talk to God
I know my cry He heard

If this is what they call healing
It is harder than I thought
It is not over the counter
It can not be store bought

When I finally walk away
From everything hurting me
I will learn to press REPEAT
NO You will NOT win
defeat!!!

And yes my lip bleeds
And yes my face hurts
And yes the bruises fade
But the roots are way worse

Of what you planted inside
But I won't water that anymore

I am still God's daughter
And He has far more in store!!!
🌹> 🔲

"Draw near to God and He will draw near to you."

-James 4:8 (NKJV)

Hotline to Heaven

Father God,
And Captain of ALL Seas
Tonight I humbly
Bow my knee

In the privacy of my room
I don't cry out to the moon
Lord I simply
Look to YOU

Because You delivered me from cancer
So I've experienced death to LIFE
"Greater is He" mentality
Resides on my inside

But this evening I'm struggling
So I only call on You
Spirit of the Living God
Do what only You can do

Move me
Shift me
Speak a word
And I will go

Let me kill my flesh
So in your image I can grow

With every day that passes
I know I NEED You more
You kept me here for a reason
Now reveal what it is for

Hotline to Heaven
But I've been on hold so long
Holy Spirit have your way
I'm ready for a new song

Lord release the pain
That is drippin off of me
Satan loose your chains
I'm a daughter of the King!!!

Sick and tired of sick and tired
There's Another in the Fire
Jesus went before
So that I could be rewired

Free from addiction
Free from pain
Free from daddy issues
Free from the drain

Of bottles that won't fill you
And men whose words will kill you
Because something died in them

Before you ever came along

Hotline to Heaven
Help me sing a new song

Father God I'm cryin out
Humbly on my knees
Hotline to Heaven
Who have You have called me to be?

I wanna be better
I wanna do better
I wanna pray better
I wanna live better
I wanna love better
I wanna give better
I wanna make a book
Outta all my love letters

I wanna know You more
And answer when you call
I wanna know your voice
So that next time I don't fall

I wanna create something on Earth
That resembles Heaven on every floor
I guess that's why you put music in my heart
To dance with the children and open all the doors

That NO man can shut
Because there's favor on my life
Hell should tremble
Whenever I pass by

God gives me strength
And won't let me break
Unless it's breakthrough
To hold something new

Wisdom leaking in
Deposits have been sent
Sealed and signed with grace
I've been marked by His trace

Triggers

ጸ

As I sit here
And realize
All the pain
That's locked inside
Of people busy
Tryna hide
From this & that
And their own lives
It's funny how
We compromise
For those
Who we don't even like
devils dancin
In disguise
But somehow breakin
Makes us wise
Rather stand for somethin
Then sit or lie
Been fightin for so long
I should win a prize
And even though
I tend to cry
Nothing is worth suicide!!!
Pick up the pieces
Put down the pride

Pay attention to the triggers
Cuz they are the guides
Follow the word
He's still on your side
Maybe it's time I finally abide
Obedience is key
So open up wide
Get still baby cuz here comes the tide
Surrender it all and enjoy the ride
Cuz it don't stop for you or I

Tiffany

☀

If diamonds are formed
Under the greatest pressure
Then she shines the brightest
You cannot 4get her
1 day you'll regret her
Or let her
Just let hurt
Breeze right past her way
"Lack of effort
Got me rapping different"
At least that's what Drake say
So press harder
Transform it
There's beauty in pain
There's lessons & blessings
Aggression & tears
There's walls and there's chains
We must break after years
Of swimmin
And drownin
And losin our way
I thank God 4 each night
4 my life every day
While they're swipin & fightin
I'm readin & writin

Simplicity meant for me
Stop all the hypin
Of things that don't matter
Can't hear in the chatter
Rewritin my chapter
I keep runnin faster
A "keeper" or crasher?
And no you can't have her!
No test drives in life
So go hard or go home
Never the 1/2 way type
So I'm whole all alone
I don't like whatevers
I DO trust myself
Call me Tiffany baby
Soul's drippin in wealth

#preciousstone

Love You Twice

ℛ

If you're getting
this poem tonight
It's because
you mean something in my life
If I loved you once
Then I love you twice
Never played it safe
Always rolled the dice
Not on who
I thought was nice
But the leaders of tomorrow
Who fight for what's right
Not the cool kid table
The loners who bite
And chew off more
Than what's in sight
Who take the heat
While they chase the light
And face every hardship
with delight
The dreamers who dream
I hold onto tight
Cuz you changed my script
to YES from "I might"
Make me believe

We can reach new heights
Woke up the inner child
Let's go fly kites!
On a serious note,
I'd even take a flight
Cuz my faith in humanity
is restored by your light :)

Daisy

Collect you some people
Who make you feel like magic
Leave you a little lighter
Than when you arrived
With all your baggage
I swear this life of mine
Has been a little savage
But then you meet your tribe
And you're happy that you had it
Cuz it makes you who you are
I guess there's beauty in the struggle
Everything builds up inside
Until you pop just like a bubble
In my art there's never pride
Just love and pain that's doubled
You can feel it in my eyes
Memories run right down like puddles
So I MASTER every PIECE
Even though my moves are subtle
Snowflakes fall right from the tree
I think I found my team
Let's huddle
Quality over quantity
Brings a lot less trouble
So make a movie

Take a picture
Cuz I am one for the books
Wrap you up in my Daisy chains
If you get a second look

Another

ঙ

What am I healing?
Don't even know what I'm feeling
Sober Saturday evening
Look up at my ceiling

I should be kneeling
Giving thanks for the peeling
Layers come off
After all of my dealings

Life sent me reeling
Like off road 4 wheeling
Now all I want is LOVE
After drinking and mealing

Of course God willing
Should I wake tomorrow
But only the real kind
I never like borrowed

Had enough sorrow
through all the transitions
Keep prayin to my Father
Maybe it's time to listen

So break me and bruise me
But let me recover
Ready for the mission
To be light for another

Inside

ℛ

And sometimes I wish
I would've been good
@justonething
Instead of scattered pieces
Aftermath of my remains
So I watch
And I listen
And I smell
And I taste
I try to remind myself
That nothing is a waste
I touch every place that hurts
So I know where to BEGIN
We break
We bruise
We burn
We learn to START again
I'm beginning to believe
I'm my own treasured friend
Finding LOVE inside these walls
Where my body used to sin
Spirit singing out of me

I am happy
I am free
So while you're out there
Lookin 4 the world
I found the world
Inside of ME

"Me Time"

At the end of each night
When the world switches off
Her soul could just land
On a cloud that was soft
She realized that wandering
Didn't make her lost
Cuz in her own planet
She was a BOSS
No not that kind
That comes to your mind
More like the sweetest
Bottle of SunShine
You know the typa girl
Who can't be defined
She liked coloring books
But outside of the lines
Not even couture
was fit to design
A heart that's so pure
No need to refine
So she just did her
Mixed with some wine
Creative head to toe
Think she needs a warning sign
Work in Progress

Isn't just a rhyme
Love the nights to just dream
Guess I call it "me time"

#blackandwhite #backtobasics #writer #poet
#artist #daythinker #nightdreamer

Unfinished Human

Ⴤ

Unfinished Human
That's what I am
A constant work in progress
Just working on His plan

The sunrise after darkness
The music after noise
The laughter after tears
God's grace gives me poise

I Like

ༀ

I like a life without rules
I like people who are real
I like speaking of my dreams
I like music that heals
I like food that is warm
I like dancing in the rain
I like wine that is chilled
I like forgetting my pain
I like the laugh of a child
I like learning what I don't know
I like my heart young
I like my old soul
I like that I still love
I like who I could be
I like who I'm becoming
I like that I am free

29

ꙮ

Sittin here alone
Reflectin on life
The last few years
Cut me open like a knife
Some may call me damaged goods
But the cracks led to the light
That will help a generation
Looks like I'm the Nation's wife
We can heal
We can heal
Lift it up
And just stay real
Always fightin for the people
Who can't fight for themselves
Little sunshine and a good song
Always seems to help
Keep your money and your titles
Health's the greatest form of wealth
So let the water pour
Cleanse the mind
Release your soul
God's the only answer
To how I filled my hole
So use me, use me!!!
Don't let it go to waste

"What I been through
Probly offend you"
At least that's what Kendrick say
For the 1st time
In a long time
I can finally see the way
Close my eyes and felt my heartbeat poundin love, and grace and faith
So quiet those tears
Talk back to those fears
Im standin in my purpose
After 29 years

Heal Nations

ዩ

He said,
Right now I want you single
Cuz you're gonna heal Nations
Trust me baby girl
There's no time for relation-ships
Can I give you a tip?
You were made to drip
The drops of LOVE
From your lips

#bepatient #Godsplan

Mama Bear

There ain't nothin more special
Than the bond that we share
Like a package marked in "FRAGILE" 🎁
Built to handle with care
Been through every bumpy ride
But I know you're still there
You're my heart ❤ in human form
#1 Mama Bear

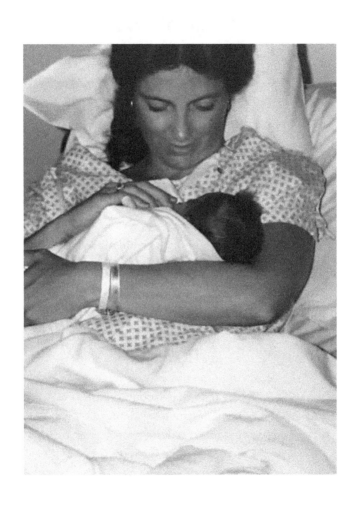

Rear View

℟

VERSE 1
There's no more lookin in the rear view
I'm livin like I'm brand new
Lovin like I'm sposed to
We got 1 life
Let's GO boots!!!

Walkin with my head high
These scars don't make me feel shy
Tell that cancer goodbye
Cuz it's my time to
Fly-y

[CHORUS]
And I'm gonna fly away
From the pain that's groundin me
Said I'm gonna fly away
Trading in my old broken wings
And I'm gonna fly away
Cuz there's still so much to see
Said I'm gonna fly away
I can do it with you next to me

I can do it with ya next to me
I can do it with ya next to me
I can do it with you next to me
I can do it with you next to me

REPEAT

*"Therefore, if anyone is in Christ, the new creation has
come: The old has gone, the new is here!"*

-2 Corinthians 5:17 (NIV)

It's Never Too Late Too...

❧

It's never too late
To give
It's never too late
To try
It's never too late
To live
Her heart whispered,
"I'm not ready to die"

It's never too late
To dream
It's never too late
To seem
Like you're more than what you are
So she set her sights up far

It's never too late
To hope
It's never too late
To joke
I could use a laugh or two
I've cried until my tears are through

It's never too late
For love

It's never too late
For hugs
Touch me til the pain is gone
I've been travelin
For so long

It's never too late
For wine
It's never too late
To make time
Throw a record on that takes me away
Reminds me to smile
And makes me stay

It's never too late
To forgive the past
It's never too late
To remove the mask

It's never too late
To say I need help
It's never too late
To feel what I felt

It's never too late
To start over again
It's never too late
Because The Author's
My friend

It's never too late
Because God is ALWAYS on time
It's never too late
To say "hello sunshine"

#HeKnowsMyName #HeCallsMeFriend #AuthorAndTheFinisher

Closing Note To the Readers:

10 YEAR CHALLENGE - Write a Letter to your Future Self in 10 Years

Today is Thursday October 13, 2016. The time is 8:57AM. I sit here quietly before my computer in front of an old sun filled glass window in a cozy Georgia home. I find myself clear, calm, collected, and focused for the first time in a long time. As I sip my coffee (the way my Greek friends taught me, slowly... :) I can't help but to contemplate the end of my trip and the beginning of my life.

October is an interesting month on a lot of levels. It is considered the second month of Fall and the beginning of manifestation. The air becomes crisp and cool. The smell of cinnamon swirls through the streets, the leaves begin to change into bright vibrant colors of golden yellow, apple red and copper orange. You can feel the world around you begin to change in an instant.

October was also my Grandma Nina's favorite time of year, which makes me smile on a sentimental level :) She was one strong lady!!! I must admit, I am personally not a fan of the cold weather but this particular month has grown on me, especially living in New York City.

Getting to experience the beauty of Central Park, childlike fun of pumpkin picking upstate and adult costume parties downtown has all enhanced my appreciation for change in seasons.

Above all though… I now pause in October to salute my fellow Breast Cancer Sisters.

As I sat from the top of the rocky mountains in Positano overlooking the most breathtaking views of my life, got skylifeted over the charming city of Capri, walked through the historical ruins of Rome, danced beneath the Colosseum, skipped up the Spanish steps, sailed the seas of Athens, bathed in the Mediterranean salt, tasted every sip of wine and cheese, stopped counting carbs, indulged in pasta and gelato, embraced conversations with strangers, remembered to breathe, allowed myself to laugh and cry and finally attempt to get home with a bus, ferry and train…I must say it has been the adventure of a lifetime and a long way from where I was this time last year.

The funny thing about leaving is that you always run into yourself again (at least that's what my Mama always says). Sometimes we need to create some distance though so we can regain perspective. My lens on life has shifted dramatically. It's like for the first time ever I know what matters…what actually *really* matters.

A while back a very dear childhood friend of mine, Vika told me to write a letter to my future self in 10 years. At the time I was not ready to do this because I had no clue what I wanted to do or who I wanted to be ten years from now. Especially considering the fact that this time last year, my entire world was upside down. Today I am ready.

I simply want to be a reflection of all the things that I thought would break me and did NOT. I want to be a vessel of expression, inspiration and hope. I want to write, speak, sing, make music, dance, educate people, spark the minds of the youth and be a blessing to the elderly who have given me wisdom to carry on. But most of all… I want to love and I want to be loved.

My life was almost taken and yet in some strange way I came to realize in time that I wasn't really living at all until I found Christ, or maybe He found me. He was patient with my process and now I'm faithful with my progress. I want to dedicate the rest of my life towards working to serve Him and build the kingdom to pay it forward. Our purpose is so much greater than our position and that is what drives me every single day.

In the future I dream to open Liv Strong Studios House of Healing because I truly believe my family, friends, faith and hitting the floor again floor brought me home when I was in the wilderness and I'd like to open my doors to others in the same way. I have experienced indescribable peace in the middle of life's many storms that is so supernatural and worthy of sharing with my brothers and sisters. Until I can afford the space I will continue to have the say and turn the leftover noise in my head into a beautiful symphony and poetry book someday. When we release our pain it is no longer ours to carry. May we all let our tests become our testimonies and keep moving forward with grooves and grace because if there's one thing my dance family taught me along the way it is that

The Show Must gO On!

Cheers to the Autumn Leaves...I'm ready for a new season!!!

Yours Truly...See ya in 10 years

Love,

Olivia
www.olivialivstrong.com
olivialivstrong@gmail.com

Meet The Author

"The Show Must gO On" is a deeply intimate and personal glimpse into the window of a young woman's soul who has spent the last 30 years fighting for her dreams, love, and most recently... her life. Olivia is an accomplished dancer, entertainer, teacher and Breast Cancer Survivor who has been featured on multiple platforms at a high level but falling to her knees is what truly caused her to look up. "Unfortunately or fortunately we must get broken to become open for the light to shine through again sometimes." -Olivia

Olivia's poetry captures the highs and lows of life's many hardships in New York City as a struggling artist, woman, young cancer patient, friend, lover and family member who has dealt with a variety of challenging issues including disease, addiction, relationships, abandonment, abuse and the inner conflict of choosing faith over fear.

Her words are sweet and sensitive but also deeply thought provoking. She is relatable to anyone who may be experiencing suffering and inspiring to those who have lost hope along the way.

Truly a spiritual journey to read her verbal choreography.